Instant Vortex Air Fryer Oven Dishes

A Transforming Guide On Fast And Easy Instant Vortex Air Fryer Oven Recipes For Beginners And Advanced Users To Master The Instant Vortex Air Fryer Oven Cooking

Dana Sanders

Table of Content

INTRODUCTION **8**

AIR FRYING BASICS 8

FEATURES AND FUNCTIONS 9

TIPS FOR COOKING IN AN AIR-FRYER 11

BEST USE OF AN INSTANT VORTEX AIR-FRYER 11

MEAL PLAN 12

MEASUREMENT CONVERSION AND TIME CHARTS 13

CHAPTER NO 1: AIR-FRYER BREAKFAST RECIPES **16**

1.   COCONUT AND BLUEBERRY CHIA PUDDING RECIPE 16

2.   BACON AND EGG AIR-FRYER BREAKFAST PASTRIES RECIPE 18

3.   LENTILS AND POACHED EGGS RECIPE 20

4.   SOFT-BOILED EGGS RECIPE 23

5.   TRAIL MIX OATMEAL RECIPE 24

6.   SAUCY PINTO BEANS RECIPE 26

7.   PUMPKIN SPICE STEEL-CUT OATS 29

8.   BROCCOLI-CHEDDAR EGG MUFFINS RECIPE 31

CHAPTER NO: 2 LUNCH **34**

9.   AIR-FRIED BUTTERMILK CHICKEN 34

10. COPYCAT KFC POPCORN CHICKEN IN THE AIR-FRYER 37

11.   AIR-FRYER LEMON PEPPER CHICKEN BREAST.......................................39

CHAPTER NO: 3 DINNER RECIPES 42

12.   AIR FRIED PEPPERONI WRAPS...42

13.   AIR-FRYER BEEF JERKY 44

14.   AIR-FRYER TRUFFLE FRIES 46

CHAPTER NO 4: AIR-FRYER POULTRY, BRUNCH RECIPES...................... 48

15.   CRISPY RANCH AIR-FRYER NUGGETS 48

16.   AIR-FRYER HONEY-CAJUN CHICKEN THIGHS 50

17.   AIR-FRYER BACON-WRAPPED CHICKEN THIGHS 52

18.   BAKED THAI PEANUT CHICKEN EGG ROLLS..54

19.   FRENCH ONION CHICKEN BREAST WITH FONTINA CHEESE 56

20.   CHICKEN PATTIES WITH GARLIC AIOLI 58

CHAPTER NO 5: AIR-FRY BEEF, MEAT AND PORK RECIPES................... 60

21.   AIR-FRYER PORK CHOPS..60

22.   PORK CHOPS BREADED IN CRUSHED ALMONDS AND PARMESAN............62

23.   AIR-FRYER GLAZED PORK CHOPS 64

24.   CRISPY FRIED PORK CHOPS...65

25.   AIR-FRYER PORK RIND BREADING CHOPS..68

26.   GARLIC PARMESAN PORK CHOPS..70

CHAPTER NO 6: AIR-FRYER FISH AND SEAFOOD RECIPES 72

27. THAI STYLE FISH FILLET 72

28. AIR FRIED YELLOW CROAKER FISH 75

29. KIMCHI AND CHEESE BAKED FISH 77

30. AIR-FRYER BAJA FISH TACOS 79

31. AIR-FRYER SOUTHERN FRIED CATFISH 82

32. AIR-FRYER CRAB STUFFED MUSHROOMS 85

CHAPTER NO 7: AIR-FRYER APPETIZERS, BREAD AND SNACKS............ 88

33. AIR-FRYER SRIRACHA-HONEY CHICKEN WINGS RECIPE.......88

34. AIR-FRYER CHEESY GARLIC BREAD 90

35. AIR-FRYER FIVE CHEESE PULL-APART BREAD 91

36. QUICK PARMESAN DUSTED GARLIC KNOTS 93

37. AIR BAKED BUTTERY DINNER ROLLS 95

38. AIR-FRYER PIZZA HUT BREAD STICKS 97

CHAPTER NO 8: AIR-FRYER DESSERT AND FRITTATAS RECIPES 100

39. AIR-FRYER TWIX CHEESECAKE 100

CHAPTER NO 9: AIR-FRY VEGETABLES & SIDES RECIPES.................... 104

40. ZUCCHINI PARMESAN CHIPS 104

CONCLUSION.. 108

Introduction

Air frying utilizes superheated cooling air instead of hot oil to create the same crunchy flavor and feel deep-fried food. It always traps juices within the crispy covering, except without the extra grease: it's faster, lighter, better, and a lot less effort.

Air fry, bake, roast, and reheat in a flash with the pre-programmed Smart Programs. Juicy chicken wings, crispy fries, onion rings, and more are all air fried. Cauliflower bites, garlicky peas, shrimp skewers, and chicken nuggets are roasted in the fryer, Calzones or mini pizzas baked in the fryer, soft cinnamon rolls baked in the oven, and chewy brownie bits baked in the oven. Alternatively, for lunch, reheat last night's meal.

Air Frying Basics

What is an air-fryer, and how does it work?

Air-fryers are tiny countertop convection ovens in their most common form. They easily heat a tiny internal basket to high temperatures. They even have a fan that circulates hot air around the cooking basket at a fast level.

What are the benefits of using an air-fryer for cooking?

1. Air trying is a safer method of cooking.

Food fried in an air-fryer is so much healthier than food cooked in a deep fat fryer. You can cook your food with little or no oil.

2. Air frying is a quick way of cooking.

The air-fryer's convection fan rapidly circulates superheated air around the cooking. Cooking will be 20-30% easier than utilizing a standard oven as a result of this.

3. Air frying will help you save money and electricity.

When you turn on the daily oven, you're heating a massive cavernous cooking space.

Air-fryers heat up faster, need less space to retain heat, and cool off faster because of the limited internal cooking space. As a consequence, the amount of electricity used is normally reduced.

An air-fryer may be a convenient and practical way to cook, heat, and reheat for those who do not have a full kitchen option.

It isn't to suggest that air-fried foods aren't delicious or crisp.

Features And Functions

How do air-fryers work?

The air-fryer isn't the same as a traditional fryer. That's the same as cooking in the oven. It does not prepare food as effectively as slow cooking or pan-frying.

Many versions do not need preheating, saving time and allowing food to be prepared quickly. They won't heat the kitchen as much as the oven would in hotter climates and temperatures.

What should be looked for in an air-fryer?

Unlike pressure cookers, air-fryers' sales will not be dominated by a single brand, such as Instant Pot. There are a few parameters and factors to keep in mind if you're looking for the best air-fryer for you.

Packing: Some versions have front drawers for loading and unloading the food, while others have a flip-top lid. Experts prefer drawer-style models for ease of use and security.

The user-friendliness: Is it easy to learn and use the controls? Perhaps you want the whole family to use an air-fryer. It should also be easy to remove and clean the basket.

Controls are essential. Most versions can be adjusted to temperatures up to 400 degrees Fahrenheit F, but some only have one. For leftovers, often people use a reheat button, as well as presets for chicken and fish.

Functionality: Is it possible to interrupt the cooking process to transform or stir the food? For certain iterations, the time and temperature must be reset.

Dimensions: Many countertop models are big enough for one or two people. If you're cooking with a large group, you'll need to make several batches or buy a larger model, which takes up a lot of space. Some models combine an air-fryer and a toaster oven, enabling you to conserve room by replacing the toaster oven.

Tips for Cooking in an Air-Fryer

- Stop overcrowding the basket to ensure even cooking. Overcrowding the basket increases the amount of time it takes to cook.

- Since the appliance has already been heated, the second batch can cook a little faster when cooking in batches!

- To stop burning and search for doneness, shake the vegetables at least halfway through cooking.

- To protect the outside of the fish from drying out, cook it at a lower temperature than recommended.

- Put skin side up for crispy skin. The top of an air-fryer heats up.

Best Use of An Instant Vortex Air-Fryer

It's easy to use, and it's also quick to vacuum. It comes with a maintenance guide and a security guidance manual. The cooking tray blends into the bottom of the air-fryer basket.

It was lightweight and easy to drive around. It's recommended that you leave at least 5" of space around the Instant Air-fryer.

The Vortex has Smart Programs, which have preset temperatures and cooking times.

Chips, chicken nuggets, cauliflower wings, and more can be air fried.

Bake light and fluffy cookies and pastries, scalloped potatoes, and more.

Roasted meat, pork, vegetables, fish, and more.

To serve leftovers, heat it without drying it out or overcooking it.

Broil for top-down cooking, melt cheese around nachos and serve with a French onion soup.

It should be dehydrated.

You may adjust the time or temperature of air frying without stopping the process. To set the time or temperature for cooking, press the Time or Temp button and rotate the dial until it clicks.

Meal Plan

This Air-fryer meal plan is designed to make your life EASY.

Once you try meal planning, you will never want to go back. Need more convincing? Here are just a few ways you will benefit from following this meal plan:

- Shopping for groceries is more effective. There will be no more last-minute runs to the supermarket for the evening's dinner.

- It helps you save time. You will avoid all the regular choices on what to make by planning ahead of time.

- Reduces waste by avoiding the need to purchase more ingredients at the store.

- Since they will help select the weekly meal plan order, the whole family is interested. They can also chip in and assist in the kitchen so that they know what's for dinner.

- It's interesting to learn new stuff. You will arrange some creativity and have fun preparing more "fresh to you" recipes if you plan your meals ahead of time.

Measurement Conversion and Time Charts

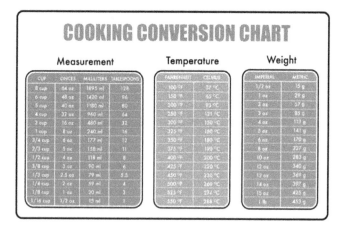

	Temperature (°F)	Time (min)		Temperature (°F)	Time (min)
Vegetables					
Asparagus (sliced 1-inch)	400°F	5	Onions (pearl)	400°F	10
Beets (whole)	400°F	40	Parsnips (½-inch chunks)	380°F	15
Broccoli (florets)	400°F	6	Peppers (1-inch chunks)	400°F	15
Brussels Sprouts (halved)	380°F	15	Potatoes (small baby, 1.5 lbs)	400°F	15
Carrots (sliced ½-inch)	380°F	15	Potatoes (1-inch chunks)	400°F	12
Cauliflower (florets)	400°F	12	Potatoes (baked whole)	400°F	40
Corn on the cob	390°F	6	Squash (½-inch chunks)	400°F	12
Eggplant (1½-inch cubes)	400°F	15	Sweet Potato (baked)	380°F	30 to 35
Fennel (quartered)	370°F	15	Tomatoes (cherry)	400°F	4
Green Beans	400°F	5	Tomatoes (halves)	350°F	10
Kale leaves	250°F	12	Zucchini (½-inch sticks)	400°F	12
Mushrooms (sliced ¼-inch)	400°F	5			
Chicken					
Breasts, bone in (1.25 lbs.)	370°F	25	Legs, bone in (1.75 lbs.)	380°F	30
Breasts, boneless (4 oz.)	380°F	12	Wings (2 lbs.)	400°F	12
Drumsticks (2.5 lbs.)	370°F	20	Game Hen (halved - 2 lbs.)	390°F	20
Thighs, bone in (2 lbs.)	380°F	22	Whole Chicken (6.5 lbs.)	360°F	75
Thighs, boneless (1.5 lbs.)	380°F	18 to 20	Tenders	360°F	8 to 10
Beef					
Burger (4 oz.)	370°F	16 to 20	Meatballs (3-inch)	380°F	10
Filet Mignon (8 oz.)	400°F	18	Ribeye, bone in (1-inch, 8 oz.)	400°F	10 to 15
Flank Steak (1.5 lbs.)	400°F	12	Sirloin steaks (1-inch, 12 oz.)	400°F	9 to 14
London Broil (2 lbs.)	400°F	20 to 28	Beef Eye Round Roast (4 lbs.)	390°F	45 to 55
Meatballs (1-inch)	380°F	7			

	Temperature (°F)	Time (min)		Temperature (°F)	Time (min)
Pork and Lamb					
Loin (2 lbs.)	360°F	55	Bacon (thick cut)	400°F	6 to 10
Pork Chops, bone in (1-inch, 6.5 oz.)	400°F	12	Sausages	380°F	15
Tenderloin (1 lb.)	370°F	15	Lamb Loin Chops (1-inch thick)	400°F	8 to 12
Bacon (regular)	400°F	5 to 7	Rack of lamb (1.5 - 2 lbs.)	380°F	22
Fish and Seafood					
Calamari (8 oz.)	400°F	4	Tuna steak	400°F	7 to 10
Fish Fillet (1-inch, 8 oz.)	400°F	10	Scallops	400°F	5 to 7
Salmon, fillet (6 oz.)	380°F	12	Shrimp	400°F	5
Swordfish steak	400°F	10			
Frozen Foods					
Onion Rings (12 oz.)	400°F	8	Fish Sticks (10 oz.)	400°F	10
Thin French Fries (20 oz.)	400°F	14	Fish Fillets (½-inch, 10 oz.)	400°F	14
Thick French Fries (17 oz.)	400°F	18	Chicken Nuggets (12 oz.)	400°F	10
Mozzarella Sticks (11 oz.)	400°F	8	Breaded Shrimp	400°F	9
Pot Stickers (10 oz.)	400°F	8			

Chapter No 1: Air-Fryer Breakfast Recipes

1. Coconut and Blueberry Chia Pudding recipe

Cook Time: 15 mins Servings: 2 Difficulty: Easy

Ingredients

- 160 g chia seeds 400 degrees ml full fat coconut milk

- Fresh berries for garnish optional

- 240 ml water 1/2 tsp pure vanilla extract

- 340 g frozen blueberries

- 90 g rolled oats

- 160 g pure maple syrup

Instructions

1. In the inner cup, mix the water, coconut milk, chia seeds, blueberries, maple syrup, oats, and vanilla extract.

2. Cover the lid and lock it. Choose Pressure Cook or Manual, and set the pressure to high for 3 mins. After frying, let the pressure naturally relax for 5 mins before immediately removing any residual pressure.

3. Break the lid by opening it. Refrigerate the pudding in small serving cups for 1 hour or before it sets.

4. Serve cold with berries on top, or seal tightly and store in the refrigerator for up to 4 days.

2. Bacon and Egg Air-fryer Breakfast Pastries Recipe

Cook Time: 15 mins Servings: 4 Difficulty: Easy

Ingredients

- 4 slices of bacon cooked and crumbled

- 225 g sheet frozen puff pastry

- Finely chopped parsley or chives for garnish

- 85 g grated cheddar cheese

- 4 eggs

Instructions

1. Thaw and open puff pastry according to box guidance on a thinly floured board, then cut into four squares.

2. Pick Air Fryer and set the temperature to 388 degrees F for over simple eggs (or up to 15 mins for fully fried

eggs), then hit the eggs. Starting preheating the Vortex.

3. After 5 mins, use a metal spoon, push down each pastry's middle to create a nest, and be cautious not to collapse the edges.

4. 1/4 of the cheese should be pushed to the left to line the nest, and 1/4 of the fried bacon should be sprinkled along the sides.

5. Transfer the cooking drawer to the Vortex and gently break an egg into each of the nests.

6. When the cooking time is over, check the eggs and see whether they are cooked to your taste.

7. Repeat measures 2–8 for the remaining two pastry squares.

8. Garnish with chopped parsley or chives and serve hot.

3. Lentils and Poached Eggs Recipe

Cook Time: 19 mins Servings: 4 Difficulty: Medium

Ingredients

- 1 tbsp finely chopped fresh parsley

- 1 lemon Grated zest and juice

- 3/4 cup dried brown or green lentils rinsed and drained

- 1/4 tsp black pepper

- 2 dried bay leaves

- 4 cups baby spinach

- 3 cups Water divided

- 4 eggs

- 3 tbsp extra-virgin olive oil

- 1/2 tsp salt divided

- Nonstick cooking spray

Instructions

1. In the Instant Pot, combine the lentils, bay leaves, and 2 cups of water. Set the Pressure Cook button to 7 mins after sealing the cap and closing the valve.

2. Meanwhile, whisk together the parsley, oil, lemon zest & juice, and 1/4 teaspoon salt in a shallow cup. Remove from the equation.

3. Cooking Spray over 4 ramekins and smash 1 egg into every ramekin. Remove from the equation.

4. Quickly relieve the strain. Carefully lift the cap and drain the lentils as the valve drops. Return the spinach, lentils, and 1/4 teaspoon of salt to the Air-fryer. Toss until the spinach is scarcely wilted, then split into four soup bowls. To stay warm, cover.

5. 1 cup water, a trivet, and 3 ramekins should be added to the pot. Stack the 4th ramekin on top of

the others. Reset the Pressure Cook button to 1 minute after sealing the lid, removing the valve, and clicking the Cancel button.

6. Using a one-minute natural pressure release followed by a fast pressure release. Carefully remove the lid until the valve has fallen. Remove the ramekins from the oven and drain any extra water that has been collected throughout the cooking process. To quickly remove the eggs from the ramekin, carefully loop a knife along the outside edges of each shell.

7. Top every serving of lentils with an equal quantity of the oil mixture and the eggs. Season with black pepper to taste.

4. Soft-boiled Eggs Recipe

Cook Time: 2 mins Servings: 2 Difficulty: Easy

Ingredients

- Multiple eggs on the trivet

- 250 ml water

Instructions

1. Fill the inner pot halfway with water, then carefully put the eggs on the trivet within.

2. Low pressure for almost 2 mins, then Fast Pressure Release is programmed.

3. Serve immediately.

5. Trail Mix Oatmeal Recipe

Cook Time: 10 mins Servings: 2 Difficulty: Easy

Ingredients

- 1 tbsp dried cranberries

- 1 tbsp raisins

- 1 cup steel-cut oats

- pinch of salt

- 1 1/2 cups water

- 2 tbsp chopped pecans

- 1 tsp butter

- 1/4 tsp ground cinnamon

- 1 cup Freshly Squeezed Orange Juice

- 1 tbsp chopped dried apricots

- 1 tbsp pure maple syrup

Instructions

1. In the Instant Pot, combine both of the ingredients. Stir all together in a mixing dish. Close the door.

2. Set the timer to 10 mins by clicking the Manual keys. When the timer beeps, release pressure rapidly before the float valve decreases, then open the lid.

3. Oatmeal can be stirred. Divide the cooked oats evenly on two plates. Heat the dish before serving.

6. Saucy Pinto Beans Recipe

Cook Time: 15 mins Servings: 2 Difficulty: Easy

Ingredients

- 225 g passata

- 1/2 tsp salt

- 2 bay leaves

- 1/2 tsp black pepper

- 1 medium jalapeño seeded & diced

- 1 tsp cumin

- 1 tsp minced Garlic

- 1 tsp dried oregano

- 800 ml vegetable stock

- 1 big yellow onion, diced

- 450 g dry pinto beans

- 1 tbsp chili powder

- 2 tbsp avocado oil

- 1 tbsp yellow mustard

Instructions

1. Fill a bowl of 3 inches of water and apply the beans. Soak the beans for 4–8 hrs before cooking. The beans should be drained.

2. Add the oil to the Instant Pot and press the Sauté handle. Add the onion, jalapeno, and garlic after the oil has heated for 1 minute. Sauté for around 5 mins, or before softened.

3. In the inner pot, combine the soaked beans, mustard, stock, chili powder, bay leaves, passata, oregano, pepper, cumin, and salt. Stir all together thoroughly, scraping some brown bits off the bottom of the kettle. Close the door.

4. Switch the time to 25 mins by clicking the Pressure Cook handle.

5. Once the timer goes, let the pressure naturally escape before the float valve decreases, then open the lid.

6. After cutting and discarding the bay leaves, move the beans to a serving dish.

7. Pumpkin spice steel-cut oats

Cook Time: 15 mins Servings: 5 Difficulty: Easy

Ingredients

Dry ingredients

- 1/4 cup brown sugar

- 1/2 cups steel cut oats

- 1/2 cup roughly chopped walnuts

- 1 tbsp Pumpkin Pie Spice

- 1/2 tsp sea salt

- 1/2 cup raisins

For cooking and serving

- 1 cup pumpkin purée 6 cups water

Instructions

1. In the pot, layer the dry ingredients.

2. In the Instant Cup, combine both of the jarred ingredients. 6 cups water, plus the pumpkin puree to combine, stir all together. Place the cover on top and make sure the vent is set to "Sealed." Cook for 15 mins on high.

3. Click the Cancel icon. Allow 10 mins for the steam pressure to escape before manually releasing the residual pressure automatically.

8. Broccoli-Cheddar Egg Muffins Recipe

Cook Time: 5 mins Servings: 7 Difficulty: Easy

Ingredients

- 1/2 tbsp cream cheese

- 3 large eggs

- 1/4 cup shredded Cheddar cheese

- 3/4 ounce wedge Laughing Cow light Swiss cheese

- 1 cup broccoli florets chopped

- 1 green onion

Instructions

1. Mix the Laughing Cow cheese and eggs in a 1-pint Mason jar with a big muzzle. Mix for about 15 secs with an immersion blender, only until smooth.

2. Fill the Instant Pot halfway with water. Grease 7 silicone muffin cups generously with sugar, making

sure to get both of the ridges. Put the cups of muffins on a steam rack with a long handle.

3. Sprinkle the green onions and broccoli equally among the muffin cups, then dump them in the egg mixture, separate it properly, and fill each midway. Cheddar cheese should be uniformly spread in the cups. Slowly put the muffin cups into the fryer when retaining the steam rack handles. Clasp the steam rack's handles together if necessary.

4. Adjust the Pressure Release to Sealing and close the lid. Set the cooking period for 8 mins at low pressure utilizing the Steam setting.

5. Allow the pressure to automatically relax for 5 mins after the cooking software has finished, then switch the Pressure Release to Venting to release any residual steam. Remove the cover from the oven. The egg muffins would have puffed up a lot during frying,

so they will deflate and relax when they cool. Catch the steam rack handles with heat-resistant mitts and pull the muffin cups out of the oven. Allow the muffins to cool for around 5 mins, or until they are cool enough to treat.

6. To extract the muffins from the muffin cups, take sides away from the muffins and pass them to plates.

Chapter No: 2 Lunch

9. Air-fried buttermilk chicken

Cook time: 18 mins Servings: 4 Difficulty: Easy

Ingredients

- 800g store-bought chicken thighs (skin on, bone-in)

Marinade

- Seasoned Flour

- 2 cups buttermilk

- 1 tbsp paprika powder

- 2 tsp black pepper

- 1 tbsp garlic powder

- 1 tsp cayenne pepper

- 1 tbsp baking powder

- 2 tsp salt

- 2 cups all-purpose flour

- 1 tsp salt

Instructions

1. Remove any visible fat and residue from the chicken thighs by rinsing them and patting them dry with paper towels.

2. In a large mixing cup, toss the chicken parts with the black pepper, paprika, and salt to cover. Put buttermilk over the chicken and toss to cover. Refrigerate for 6 hours or overnight in the fridge.

3. Preheat the Air-Fryer to 360 degrees F.

4. Combine rice, baking powder, paprika, and salt and pepper in a separate dish. Remove the chicken from the buttermilk one slice at a time and dredge in seasoned flour. Switch to a plate after shaking off the extra starch.

5. Place one sheet of chicken on the fryer basket, skin side up, and slip it into the air-fryer. Load the timer for 8 mins and air fry. Remove the tray from the oven, flip the chicken parts over, and set the timer for a further 10 mins.

6. Drain on towels before serving.

10. Copycat KFC Popcorn Chicken in the Air-Fryer

Cook time: 12 mins Servings: 12 Difficulty: Easy

Ingredients

- 60 ml Bread Crumbs

- 1 Chicken Breast

- 50 g Plain Flour

- 2 ml KFC Spice Blend

- 1 Small Egg beaten

- Salt & Pepper

Instructions

1. Blend the chicken in a food processor until it looks like a minced chicken.

2. Set up a table with a bowl filled with flour and another filled with beaten eggs. In a third dish,

combine the KFC spice mixture, salt, and pepper, followed by the bread crumbs.

3. Then roll the minced chicken into balls & roll them in rice, egg, and spiced bread crumbs like a factory line.

11. Air-Fryer Lemon Pepper Chicken Breast

Cook time: 18 mins Servings: 3 Difficulty: Easy

Ingredients

- 1 Large Lemon juice and rind

- 1 tsp Garlic Powder

- 3 Large Chicken Breasts

- 2 tsp Ground Black Pepper

- 1 Medium Lemon

- ½ tsp Sea Salt

Instructions

1. Place the chicken breasts on a cutting board that has been washed.

2. Season the chicken breasts with sea salt after smothering them in lemon juice & rind from a big

lemon.

3. Garlic powder and black pepper can be added.

4. In the Air-Fryer basket, position your chicken breasts. Cut the lemon slices and put them on top as well as to the sides of the breasts. Cook for 15 mins at 360°F in an Air-Fryer.

5. If the chicken is already pink in the center, continue cooking for another 3-5 mins. Serve the chicken breasts sliced.

Chapter No: 3 Dinner Recipes

12.   Air fried pepperoni wraps

Cook time: 20 mins Servings: 2 Difficulty: Easy

Ingredients

- 28 pepperoni slices

- 2 flour tortillas

- 2 tbsp sharp cheddar cheese

- 2 slices cooked bacon, crumbled

- 2 tbsp mozzarella cheese

Instructions

1. Arrange tortillas on a large serving platter.

2. On each tortilla, place half of the pepperoni slices in a layer.

3. On each tortilla, position 1 slice of crumbled bacon.

4. 1 tbsp mozzarella cheese on each tortilla

5. 1 tbsp sharp cheddar cheese, sprinkled over every tortilla

6. Cover it up and put it in the Air-Fryer basket, seam side down.

7. Using a butter-flavored cooking spray, coat the pan.

8. Cook for almost 3-5 mins in an Air-Fryer at 400 degrees F or until cheese melts and optimal crispiness is attained.

13.   Air-Fryer beef jerky

Cook time: 4 hrs Servings: 8 Difficulty: Easy

Ingredients

- 1-inch piece fresh ginger root, grated and peeled

- 12 ounces top sirloin beef

- 1 tbsp rice vinegar

- 1 garlic clove, minced

- 1 tbsp chili paste

- 2 tbsp reduced-sodium soy sauce

- 1 tbsp turbinado sugar

Instructions

1. Thinly slice the beef with a sharp knife and put it in a resealable jar.

2. Mix the garlic, soy sauce, ginger, chili paste, sugar, and rice vinegar in a mixing cup.

3. Place the marinade in a bag, seal it, and refrigerate for at least 4 hours or 24 hours.

4. Remove the bits of beef from the marinade and pat them dry with a paper towel until ready to serve.

5. Preheat the Air-Fryer to 320 degrees Fahrenheit. Cook for 3 to 4 hours with the beef in the basket. Check the jerky for doneness daily. Enable for full cooling before storage in the airtight jar.

14.   Air-Fryer truffle fries

Cook time: 18 mins Servings: 4 Difficulty: Easy

Ingredients

- 1⁄4 tsp kosher salt 1 1⁄4 lbs Yukon gold potatoes

- 1 tbsp olive oil 3⁄4 tsp truffle salt

Instructions

1. Scrub the potatoes and rinse them. Cut the fries into even pieces and put them in a dish.

2. Toss in the olive oil & kosher salt to cover.

3. Put the fries in the Air-Fryer basket and cook for almost 15 to 18 mins at 350 degrees F, shaking the basket halfway through. Cook until lightly browned and dry, about 10 mins.

4. Remove the fries from the Air-Fryer and quickly season with truffle salt before serving.

Chapter No 4: Air-Fryer Poultry,

Brunch Recipes

15.   Crispy Ranch Air-fryer Nuggets

Cook time: 10 mins Servings: 4 Difficulty: Easy

Ingredients

- 2 tbsp flour 1 pound chicken tenders, cut into 1 1/2 to 2-inch pieces 1 serving olive oil cooking spray

- 1 (1 ounce) package dry ranch salad dressing mix

- 1 egg, lightly beaten

- 1 cup panko bread crumbs

Instructions

1. Toss the chicken with the ranch seasoning in a large mixing dish. Allow for 5-10 mins of resting time.

2. Fill a resealable bag halfway with flour. In a tiny mug, crack an egg and spread panko bread crumbs on a tray. Preheat the air-fryer to 390 degrees F.

3. Toss the chicken in the bag to coat it. Dip the chicken in the egg mixture lightly, allowing excess to run off. Roll the chicken parts in panko crumbs, grinding them into the meat.

4. Spray the air-fryer basket with oil and arrange the chicken parts inside; make sure they don't collide. Depending on the scale of the air-fryer, you will need to do two batches. Using a light mist of cooking oil, lightly coat the chicken.

5. Cook for a total of 4 mins. Cook for another 4 mins. Serve straight away.

16. Air-fryer Honey-Cajun Chicken Thighs

Cook time: 25 mins Servings: 6 Difficulty: Medium

Ingredients

- ⅓ cup tapioca flour

- ½ cup buttermilk

- 4 tsp honey

- 1 tsp hot sauce

- ⅛ tsp cayenne pepper

- 1 ½ pound skinless, boneless chicken thighs

- ¼ tsp ground paprika

- ¼ cup all-purpose flour

- ½ tsp honey powder

- 2 ½ tsp Cajun seasoning

- ½ tsp garlic salt

Instructions

1. In a resealable plastic container, combine buttermilk and hot sauce. Marinate the chicken thighs for 30 mins.

2. In a shallow mixing cup, tapioca flour, combine flour, garlic salt, Cajun seasoning, paprika, honey powder, and cayenne pepper. Remove the thighs from the buttermilk mixture and dredge them in the starch. Remove some extra flour by shaking it off.

3. Preheat the air-fryer to 360°F.

4. Cook for 15 mins in the air-fryer basket of chicken thighs. Cook for another 10 mins, or until the chicken thighs are no longer pink in the middle and the juices run free. Take the chicken thighs from the air-fryer and drizzle 1 teaspoon honey over each one.

17. Air-fryer Bacon-Wrapped Chicken Thighs

Cook time: 25 mins Servings: 4 Difficulty: Medium

Ingredients

- ¼ tsp dried basil

- ½ stick butter softened

- 2 tsp minced garlic

- ½ clove minced garlic

- 1 ½ pounds boneless skinless chicken thighs

- ¼ tsp dried thyme ⅓ pound thick-cut bacon

- ⅛ tsp coarse salt freshly ground black pepper

Instructions

1. In a mixing dish, combine melted butter, garlic, thyme, basil, salt, and pepper. To make a butter log,

spread butter on wax paper and curl it up tightly. Put it in the fridge for 2 hours or until strong.

2. On a sheet of wax paper, lay a bacon strip flat. Garlic up the chicken leg and place it on top of the bacon. Remove the chicken leg and break it free. In the center of the chicken leg, spread 1-2 tablespoons of the cold finishing butter. One end of the bacon can be tucked into the center of the chicken leg. Roll the bacon over the chicken thigh until turning it over. Repeat for most of the thighs & bacon.

3. Preheat the air-fryer to 370 degrees F.

4. Place the chicken thighs in the air-fryer basket and cook for around 25 mins. A thermometer placed near the bone can display 165 degrees Fahrenheit.

18.   Baked Thai peanut chicken egg rolls

Cook time: 8 mins Servings: 2 Difficulty: Easy

Ingredients

- Red bell pepper julienned

- 1/2 medium carrot very thinly sliced or rib boned

- 1/8 cup Thai peanut sauce 2 egg roll wrappers

- nonstick cooking spray or sesame oil

- 1 cup rotisserie chicken shredded

- 1 ½ green onions chopped

Instructions

1. Preheat the oven to 425 degrees F or the air-fryer to 390 degrees F.

2. Put the chicken with the Thai peanut sauce in a little dish.

3. On a clean, dry board, spread out the egg roll wrappers. Arrange 1/4 of the carrot, bell pepper, and onions over the lower third of an egg roll wrapper. Half a cup of the poultry mixture can be spooned over the vegetables.

4. Using mist, dampen the wrapper's outer edges. Fold the wrapper's sides in toward the middle and curl securely.

5. Continue for the left wrappers.

6. Using nonstick cooking oil, coat the assembled egg rolls. Switch them over and paint the backs of them as well.

7. Bake the egg rolls at 390 degrees F for 6-8 mins, or until crispy and golden brown in the Air-Fryer.

8. Break-in two and serve with more Thai Peanut Sauce on the hand for dipping.

19. French onion chicken breast with fontina cheese

Cook time: 15 mins Servings: 2 Difficulty: Easy

Ingredients

- salt and pepper to taste

- 1 onion

- 2–3 ounces Fontina cheese

- 2 tbsp olive oil

- salt, and pepper to taste

- 1 tsp sugar 2 tsp olive oil

- 2 boneless, skinless chicken breast

Instructions

1. Cutting the onions into small pieces is a good place to start.

2. Put the sliced onions with the salt, sugar, Ollie oil, and pepper in a shallow cup. Then, either in the air-fryer basket or in the air-fryer pan, scatter the coated onions and cook for 5-7 mins at 350 degrees F. (Preheat the air-fryer).

3. Coat the chicken breasts in olive oil, salt, and pepper, and let them sit for a few mins. Preheat the oven to 350 degrees F and fried the chicken breast for 7-9 mins. (Preheat the air-fryer).

4. Caramelized onions go on top of the chicken.

5. Place the caramelized onions in the air-fryer for around 1-2 mins at 350 degrees F, only before the cheese is melted, on top of the sliced fontina cheese.

20. Chicken Patties with Garlic Aioli

Cook time: 12 mins Servings: 2 Difficulty: Easy

Ingredients

- 1/3 tsp black pepper

- Chicken Patties

- 1 tsp salt

- 2 lb ground chicken

- 2 tbsp fresh parsley chopped

- 1/2 Tbsp lemon juice

- 1 cup grated parmesan cheese

- 1/2 clove garlic minced

- 2 tbsp fresh parsley chopped

- 1 cup Greek Yogurt

- 2 tsp onion powder

- Garlic Aoili

- oil for spraying

- 1 tsp salt

- 1 tsp garlic powder

- 1 tsp Italian seasoning

Instructions

1. In a large mixing cup, add all of the ingredients. Form the mixture into flat patties (about 9 patties total).

2. Cook for 12 mins in an air-fryer basket at 400 degrees Fahrenheit, turning halfway through.

Chapter No 5: Air-Fry Beef, Meat and Pork Recipes

21.   Air-Fryer pork chops

Cook Time: 12 mins Servings: 8 Difficulty: Easy

Ingredients

- 1 egg

- 4-8 thin-cut pork chops

- salt and pepper, to taste

- 1/2 cup milk

- 1 packet ranch seasoning mix, dry

- 2 cup bread crumbs

Instructions

1. Preheat the Air-Fryer to 360°F.

2. In a shallow tub, whisk together the egg and season with salt and pepper. Pour in the milk. Combine ranch dressing mix and bread crumbs in a separate dish.

3. Dip pork chops one at a time into the egg mixture, then coat entirely in bread crumbs.

4. Place pork chops in the basket of Air-Fryer in batches of four at a time and spray with olive oil. Cook for 6 mins on the one hand, then switch and cook for another 6 mins. Check for crispiness and cook for an additional 2-3 mins if necessary.

22. Pork Chops breaded in crushed almonds and Parmesan

Cook Time: 14 mins Servings: 4 Difficulty: Easy

Ingredients

- 1/2 cup coarsely ground almonds

- 4 pork chops (mine were 3/4" thick)

- Salt and Pepper

- 1 egg beaten

- 1/2 cup parmesan, grated

Instructions

1. In a mug, whisk together the egg and put it aside.

2. Combine the parmesan and ground almonds in a mixing dish.

3. Our pork chops will be seasoned with salt and pepper before being dipped in the beaten egg mixture.

4. Cover both surfaces of the pork chop with the almond mixture after it has been covered in egg.

5. Put the pork chops in an Instant Pot Pair or an Air-Fryer with a crisper top. Preheat the Air-Fryer to 360 degrees F and cook for 7 mins.

6. Cook for about 7 mins after flipping the pork chops. Make sure the pork hits an internal temperature of 145 degrees using a meat thermometer. Cooking time can differ depending on the thickness of the pork chop.

7. Take the pork chops from the pan and put them on a tray. Cover with aluminum foil and set aside for 5-10 mins to cool.

23.   Air-Fryer Glazed Pork Chops

Cook Time: 12 mins Servings: 4 Difficulty: Easy

Ingredients

- 1 tsp olive oil 1 tbsp Roast Vegetables & Fries Spice Blend 1 lb boneless pork chops 2 tbsp brown sugar

Instructions

- Preheat the Air-Fryer to 400 degrees F by gently spraying the basket with cooking spray.

- Brown sugar and spice mixture can be mixed.

- Rinse and pat dry pork chops. Apply a thin layer of olive oil to them. Rub the brown sugar paste evenly over all sides of the pork chops.

- Put in the Air-Fryer for a few mins. Cook for 12 mins at 400 degrees F, flipping the pork chops over after 6 mins.

24.   Crispy Fried Pork Chops

Cook Time: 20 mins Servings: 4 Difficulty: Easy

Ingredients

Pork Chops:

- 1 tsp pepper

- 4 boneless pork loin chops 1/4 to 1/2 inch thick

- 1/4 cup Buffalo Hot Sauce optional

- 1 tsp salt

- 2 cups buttermilk

Dredging Mixture:

- 1/2 cup cornstarch

- 2 tsp paprika

- 1 1/2 cups all-purpose flour

- 2 cups vegetable oil for frying

- 2 tsp salt

- 1 tsp onion powder

- 1 tsp black pepper

- 1 tsp garlic powder

Instructions

1. 1 tsp black pepper and 1 tsp salt to season pork chops

2. Stir together the buttermilk and hot sauce on a plate. Place aside the aged pork chops in the buttermilk mixture. Refrigerate for up to 6 hours before using, or use immediately.

3. Combine rice, 2 tsp cinnamon, cornstarch, paprika, onion powder, 1 tsp black pepper, and garlic powder in a small cup.

4. Remove the pork chops from the buttermilk mixture one at a time. To clear the residue, gently shake it.

Dredge it in the dredging mixture and thoroughly coat it. Remove the waste by tapping it off.

5. Place the breaded chops in a 350 degrees F oil bath. 2 or 3 chops at a time should be fried. Since the meat can lower the oil's temperature, hold it as high to 350 degrees F as possible. Fry, each slice for 4 to 5 mins on each hand, or until golden brown and the pork reaches an internal temperature of 145°F.

6. Put on paper towels after separating from the grease. Allow for a 5-minute rest period before serving.

25. Air-Fryer pork rind breading Chops

Cook Time: 17 mins Servings: 4 Difficulty: Easy

Ingredients

- 1 tsp onion powder

- 4 bone In pork chops about ¼-inch thick

- olive oil

- 1 tsp paprika

- ⅛ tsp allspice 1 tsp parsley

- 2 cups pork rinds (Finely Crushed)

- 1 tsp garlic powder

Instructions

1. Add pork rinds, paprika, parsley, garlic and onion powders, & spice to a medium bowl. Mix all together, so it's perfect.

2. Drizzle olive oil on all sides of every pork chop, making sure to coat it completely so the rinds of pork can cling to the oil.

3. Cover every pork chop absolutely in the pork rind mixture on both sides.

4. Place the pork chops in the Air-Fryer, being careful not to overcrowd them.

5. Preheat the Air-Fryer to 400 degrees F for 12 mins. When the pork chop is cooked, turn it over & cook for another 5 mins at 400 degrees F.

26.   Garlic Parmesan Pork Chops

Cook Time: 15 mins Servings: 4 Difficulty: Easy

Ingredients

- 1 tsp garlic powder

- 1/2 tbsp garlic powder

- 1/2 cup ranch dressing

- 3/4 cup panko bread crumbs

- Garlic parmesan ranch

- 1/4 cup grated parmesan cheese

- Olive oil cooking spray

- 1/4 cup grated parmesan cheese

- 4 boneless pork chops

- Kosher salt, pepper

- 1/2 tbsp italian seasoning

- 1 egg

- Pepper

Instructions

1. Combine the Italian seasoning, panko, parmesan cheese, garlic powder, kosher salt, and pepper in a shallow mixing cup. Stir before it is well combined. In a separate small dish, beat the egg with a fork when mixed.

2. Dip each pork chop in the egg, then into the panko tub, pushing the bread crumbs into both sides of the pork chops. Spray the pork chops loosely with olive oil spray before putting them in the Air-Fryer basket.

3. Preheat the Air-Fryer to 380 degrees F and cook the pork chops for 15 mins, turning halfway through and gently spraying with olive oil spray.

4. For dipping, serve with the Garlic Parmesan Ranch.

Chapter No 6: Air-Fryer Fish and

Seafood Recipes

27.   Thai Style Fish Fillet

Cook Time: 10 mins Servings: 2 Difficulty: Easy

Ingredients

- 1 tbsp minced garlic

- 2 fish fillets

- 1/2 tbsp thinly sliced basil optional

- 1 tbsp brown sugar

- 1/4 tsp red pepper flakes or to taste (optional)

- 1 tbsp oyster sauce

- 1 tsp soy sauce

- 1/2 tbsp lime juice

- 2 tsp fish sauce

Instructions

1. Put aside all of the seasoning products, except the basil.

2. Use a grill pad or a sheet of thinly greased aluminum foil to line the fryer basket.

3. Cover the fryer basket halfway with fish fillets. Brush the sauce on the fish and air fried for 8-10 mins at 400 degrees F until the fish is fried through and the surface has browned slightly. Pull the basket out and rub on more sauce every 3 mins before the fish is

cooked through, whether the fish is thicker and denser.

4. Sprinkle basil on top.

28.   Air Fried Yellow Croaker Fish

Cook Time: 15 mins Servings: 2 Difficulty: Easy

Ingredients

- 1/4 tsp salt or to taste

- 2 Yellow croaker

- 1/4 tsp white pepper powder or to taste

- 1 tbsp rice wine

- 2 tbsp corn starch

Instructions

1. Use a grill pad or a sheet of thinly greased aluminum foil to line the fryer basket.

2. For around 15 mins, marinate the fish in salt and rice wine. Meanwhile, whisk together the corn starch and white pepper powder and set aside.

3. Using a paper towel, wipe the fish off. Shake off any leftover corn starch from the trout. Place the fish in the fryer basket after spraying all sides with gasoline.

4. Air fry for 10-12 mins at 400 degrees F, flipping once in the center until the skin is crisp and light brown.

29.   Kimchi and Cheese Baked Fish

Cook Time: 10 mins Servings: 2 Difficulty: Easy

Ingredients

- 2 pieces of 5 oz Atlantic cod fillets

- pinch of salt and pepper

- 1/4 cup kimchi (chopped)

- 1/4 cup mozzarella cheese (shredded)

- 1 tbsp green onion (thinly sliced) optional

Instructions

1. Grease a pie pan or a small baking dish lightly.

2. Season the fish with salt and pepper and put it inside the pizza tub. Air fried for around 5 mins at 380 degrees F.

3. Over the tuna, scatter the sliced kimchi and finish with mozzarella cheese. For most trout, air fried for another 3 mins at 380 degrees F.

4. If needed, garnish with green onion before serving.

30.   Air-fryer Baja Fish Tacos

Cook Time: 12 mins Servings: 8 Difficulty: Easy

Ingredients

- 1/2 cup Flour (All-Purpose)

- 2 tsp Garlic Powder

- 2 pounds Mahi Mahi Filets cut into strips

- Olive Oil Sprayer

- 1 cup Milk

- Simple Corn Salsa

- 2 Limes

- Baja Fish Tacos White Sauce

- 2 large Eggs

- Shredded Cabbage

- 1 1/2 tbsp Mayonnaise

- 8 Taco Size Corn Tortillas

- 1 tsp Baking Soda

- 1/2 tsp Freshly Ground Black Pepper

- 1/2 cup Potato Starch divided

- 1 tsp Sea Salt

Instructions

1. Remove the skin from the fish and split it into 1 inch thick slices before placing it in a jar. Combine the milk and one lime juice in a mixing bowl. Set aside for 15 mins in the refrigerator.

2. In a medium mixing cup, whisk together the egg, baking soda, and mayonnaise.

3. Mix Potato Starch, Flour, and all spices in a separate dish.

4. Coat the fish in the egg mixture, and in the flour mixture, make sure that all of the bits are fully sealed. Remove some extra flour by shaking it off.

5. Refrigerate the Fish Strips for 30 mins to cool.

6. Spray the Strips generously with oil, then put the Filets, oil side down, in an Air-fryer Basket. Oil the tops of the strips liberally.

7. Cook for 7 mins at 390 degrees. Cook for an extra 5 mins after flipping the strips and spraying them with oil.

8. Place the fish on the tortillas, then top with shredded cabbage, corn salsa, and Baja Fish Tacos White Sauce. Avocado slices and a lime wedge should be included.

31.   **Air-fryer Southern Fried Catfish**

Cook Time: 13 mins Servings: 4 Difficulty: Easy

Ingredients

- Cornmeal Seasoning Mix

- Olive Oil Sprayer

- 1 cup Milk

- Silicone Basting Brush

- 1 Lemon

- 1/4 tsp Cayenne Pepper

- 1/2 cup Yellow Mustard

- 1/4 tsp Granulated Onion Powder

- 1/2 cup Cornmeal

- 1/4 tsp Chili Powder

- 1/4 cup Flour (All-Purpose)

- 1/4 tsp Freshly Ground Black Pepper

- 2 pounds Catfish Fillets

- 2 Tbsps Dried Parsley Flakes

- 1/2 tsp Kosher Salt

- 1/4 tsp Garlic Powder

Instructions

1. Add milk to the Catfish in a flat jar.

2. To produce buttermilk, cut a lemon in two and squeeze around two teaspoons of juice onto milk.

3. Refrigerate the container and soak the Fillets for 15 mins.

4. Combine the Cornmeal Seasoning Ingredients in a small dish.

5. Using paper towels, pat the Fillets dry after extracting them from the buttermilk.

6. Mustard can be generously distributed on all sides of the Fillets.

7. To make a dense covering, dip each fillet into the Cornmeal mixture and cover thoroughly.

8. Place the Fillets in an Air-fryer Basket that has been greased. Apply a generous amount of oil to the surface.

9. Cook for 10 mins at 390 degrees F. Cook for an extra 3-5 mins after flipping the Fillets and spraying them with gasoline.

32. Air-fryer crab stuffed mushrooms

Cook Time: 18 mins Servings: 7 Difficulty: Medium

Ingredients

- 2 Celery Ribs, diced pounds mushrooms (Baby Bella)

- 2 tsp Tony Chach ere's Salt Blend

- ½ cup Parmesan Cheese, shredded, divided

- ¼ Red Onion, diced

- Cooking Spray

- ½ cup Bread Crumbs (Seasoned)

- 1 tsp Hot Sauce 1 large egg

- 8 ounces Lump Crab 1 tsp Oregano

Instructions

1. Preheat the Air-fryer or the oven to 400 degrees Fahrenheit.

2. Cooking mist the Air-fryer tray. Mushroom stems can be bent. Spray the tops of the mushrooms with olive oil cooking spray. To season the mushrooms, drizzle Tony Chachere's on them. Remove from the equation.

3. Onion & celery can be diced.

4. Combine the breadcrumbs, crab, onions, egg, celery, oregano, half of the shredded Parmesan, and hot sauce in a mixing cup.

5. Cover each mushroom's interior with the filling and pile it up a bit to create a little mound.

6. Cover with the remaining shredded Parmesan.

7. In an Air-fryer, bake for 8-9 mins. Cook for 16-18 mins if using the microwave. You will need to do many batch runs depending on the scale of the Air-fryer.

Chapter No 7: Air-Fryer

Appetizers, Bread and Snacks

33.   Air-Fryer   Sriracha-Honey

Chicken Wings Recipe

Cook time: 30 mins Servings: 2 Difficulty: Easy

Ingredients

- 1 1/2 tbsp soy sauce

- 1 pound chicken wings, tips removed

- Juice of 1/2 lime

- 2 tbsp sriracha sauce

- Cilantro, chives, or scallions for garnish

- 1/4 cup honey

- 1 tbsp butter

Instructions

1. Preheat the Air-Fryer to 360 degrees Fahrenheit. Cook the chicken wings in the Air-Fryer basket for 30 mins, rotating the wings with tongs after 7 mins to ensure they are uniformly browned.

2. Add the sauce ingredients to a tiny saucepan, then bring to a boil for around 3 mins as the wings are frying.

3. When the wings are finished, toss them in a dish with the sauce until well-seasoned, then garnish with the parsley and serve right away.

34.   Air-Fryer Cheesy Garlic Bread

Cook time: 10 mins Servings: 2 Difficulty: Easy

Ingredients

- 2 tbsp butter melted 2 dinner rolls any type

- 1/2 cup grated cheese

- Garlic bread seasoning mix (fresh chopped)

Instructions

1. In a naughts-&-crosses design, cut the tops of the bread rolls off. Split as deep as you can without reaching all the way in.Fill the slits with grated cheese until both of the slits are complete, and the cheese has vanished.Brush the tops of the rolls with molten butter, then season with garlic powder.

2. Place in a 350°F Air-Fryer that has been preheated. Cook for another 5 mins, or until the cheese is fully melted.

35. Air-Fryer Five Cheese Pull-Apart Bread

Cook time: 4 mins Servings: 2 Difficulty: Easy

Ingredients

- 30 g Goats Cheese

- 30 g Mozzarella Cheese

- 1 large Bread Loaf

- 2 tsp Chives 2 tsp Garlic Puree

- 30 g Edam Cheese

- 30 g Cheddar Cheese

- 100 g Butter 30 g Soft Cheese Salt & Pepper

Instructions

1. Set aside your grated hard cheese, which can be split into four piles.

2. Melt the butter in a saucepan over medium heat. Add the garlic, chives, salt, and pepper. Cook for another 2 mins, stirring continuously. Place on the side.

3. Make little slits in your bread with a high-quality bread knife. Fill each of the small slit holes with garlic butter before both of them are done. Then, to make them a lovely creamy flavor, coat them all with soft cheese.

4. Put a little cheddar and a little goats' cheese in each one.

5. Add the Edam & mozzarella to the ones that haven't been filled yet.

6. Place the bread in the Air-Fryer for 4 mins, or until the cheese has melted and the bread is nice and toasty.

7. Serve the food.

36. Quick Parmesan Dusted Garlic Knots

Cook time: 4 mins Servings: 8 Difficulty: Easy

Ingredients

- 1 Pizza Crust (Refrigerated)

- 3 tbsp Minced Garlic

- Garlic Salt

- Parmesan Cheese Powder

- Olive Oil 3 tbsp

Instructions

1. On a cutting board, roll out the pastry.

2. Cut the dough into 14" strips.

3. Tie a knot in each strip.

4. In a cup, combine the olive oil and garlic.

5. Dip every knot in the mixture and season with a pinch of Garlic Salt.

6. Place all of the balls on a plate and place 12 at a time in the Air-Fryer.

7. Preheat the oven to 400 degrees F and cook for 4 mins.

8. When the timer goes off, open the oven, transfer to a platter, and sprinkle with Parmesan cheese before serving wet.

37.　Air Baked Buttery Dinner Rolls

Cook time: 15 mins Servings: 2 Difficulty: Easy

Ingredients

- 2 eggs

- 1 1/2 tsp Salt

- 1 cup Fresh Milk (room temperature)

- 2 1/4 tsp Instant Yeast

- 63gm Sugar

- Some Melted Butter

- 114 gm Butter (softened)

- 508 gm Bread Flour

Instructions

1. Put all of the ingredients in the bread maker pan in the order recommended by the manufacturer.

2. Select the Dough option. When the cycle is over, roll the dough out onto a gently floured surface, and then punch out the air.

3. Divide the dough into 22 pieces and roll into round balls. Place them in the Air-fryer basket, which has been lined with a baking sheet and finely oiled along the edges.

4. Cover the dough with a moist cloth and set aside for another 30 mins, or until it has approximately doubled in size.

5. Preheat the Air-fryer to 360degrees F.

6. Preheat the oven to 360°F and bake the buns for 13-15 mins, or until lightly browned.

7. When the buns have finished frying, brush them with molten butter.

38.   Air-fryer Pizza Hut Bread Sticks

Cook time: 15 mins Servings: 4 Difficulty: Easy

Ingredients

- 2 tbsp Desiccated Coconut

- 1/3 Homemade Pizza Dough

- Bread Seeds optional

- 1 tsp Garlic Puree

- 25 g Cheddar Cheese

- 1 tsp Parsley

- Salt & Pepper

Instructions

1. In a shallow saucepan, warm the coconut oil. The best method to achieve this is to cook it on low heat before it turns into a jelly. Season with salt, then pepper, and stir in the garlic puree.

2. Shape the pizza dough into a dense rectangular shape by rolling it out. Coat it with garlic oil using a cooking brush, so it is evenly covered. Sprinkle desiccated coconut on top until the garlic oil is no longer visible. Finish with a final drizzle of cheddar cheese and some bread seeds.

3. Cook for 10 mins at 360°F, then another 5 mins at 390°F, or until hot in the center and crispy on the outside in the Air-fryer.

4. When it's finished, cut it into fingers, then serve.

Chapter No 8: Air-Fryer Dessert and Frittatas Recipes

39.   Air-fryer Twix Cheesecake

Cook Time: 1 hr Servings: 12 Difficulty: Hard

Ingredients

Cookie Crust

- 1 cup Powdered Sugar

- 1 ½ cups Flour

- 1 ½ sticks Butter melted

Cheesecake

- 2 Eggs ½ package Jello Instant Cheesecake Pudding

- 1 tsp Lemon Juice

- 32 oz Cream Cheese softened

- ¼ cup Heavy Cream

- 1 ½ cup Powdered Sugar

Topping

- ⅓ cup Heavy Cream

- 3 squares Almond Bark Melting Chocolate

- 1 jar Caramel Ice-Cream Topping

Instructions

1 Using a fork, cut the cake filling into tiny sections.

2 Separate the biscuits into two layers and put them on a clean table. With a rolling pin, roll to a 4-inch circle or straighten with the fingertips.

3   Preheat the Air-fryer to 350 degrees F for 5 mins.

4   Cover each dough with filling, then pinch the sides together to seal. Make balls out of the dough.

5   Place apple pie bombs about 2 inches apart in an Air-fryer basket.

6   Cook for a further 8 mins, or until lightly browned.

7   Melt butter as the 1st batch bakes.

8   Combine the sugar & cinnamon in a mixing dish.

9   Fried apple pie bombs are dipped in melting butter on both sides.

10 Place on a wire rack after rolling in the cinnamon-sugar mixture.

11 Repeat for the rest of the ingredients.

12 Serve hot or cold, depending on your preference.

Chapter No 9: Air-Fry Vegetables

& Sides Recipes

40.   Zucchini Parmesan Chips

Cook time: 8 mins Servings: 2 Difficulty: Easy

Ingredients

- ½ cup Parmesan Cheese (grated)

- 1 egg (lightly beaten)

- Cooking spray

- 2 Zucchinis (medium-sized, thinly sliced)

- Salt & freshly cracked pepper

- ½ cup Breadcrumbs (Italian-seasoned)

- 1/2 tsp Smoked Paprika

Instructions

1. Using a knife, cut zucchinis as finely as possible. Remove extra moisture with a towel.

2. In a small dish, whisk together a drop of water, egg, and a touch of salt and pepper. Mix the grated cheese, breadcrumbs, & smoked paprika in a small dish.

3. After dipping every zucchini piece in the egg mixture, cover it with the cheese-breadcrumbs mixture. To coat, press firmly. On a wire shelf, arrange the crumb-coated slices. Repeat for the rest of the slices.

4. Using cooking oil spray to cover the crumb-coated zucchini slices.

5. Put the slices in a layer in the air-fryer basket, make sure they don't overlap.

6. Air fried for 8 mins at 350 degrees F in batches.

7. Season with salt and pepper to taste, and serve immediately with salsa or ketchup.

Conclusion

Air-fryer is simple to use and includes an integrated microprocessor for flawless output every time. It's designed to help your safe lifestyle. Enjoy all of your favorite deep-fried foods' rich tastes and crispy texture without the oil or mess. No more straining and dumping spent fryer oil—you will now have the same performance from as little as 2 tablespoons of oil. Don't give up the experience; give up the calories!

It's simple to use, clean, and maintain. It's also fast, flexible, and handy. Make all of your family's favorite fried foods without any of the mess or the regret. With the press of a button, you will enter a world of flavor.

It's easy-to-use touch controls. And since the Instant Air-fryer remembers the preferences, you can make your favorites at the click of a button.

The Instant Vortex Air-fryer is engineered to be quick, dependable, and safe, with the same dedication to safety and consumer loyalty.

The Air-fryer is a kitchen gadget that can blow the whole planet off its feet. The Air-fryer aims to offer a healthier alternative to the common yet unhealthy fried food. Except for tried turkey at Thanksgiving, most people do not fry at home, but the Air-fryer offers much versatility. It saves chefs by almost immediately heating food at a high temperature and rendering cooking a breeze.

CPSIA information can be obtained
at www.ICGtesting.com
Printed in the USA
BVHW090330040521
606332BV00006B/1130